GW01339443

For Penny and her dragons. —D.D.

For my mom. — Mau

Text © 2022 Didi Dragon
Illustrations © 2022 Maria Mau
Edited by Sirah Jarocki

No part of this book may be reproduced or transmitted in any form or by any means without written permission from the copyright holder. Your support of the author's and illustrator's rights is kind and appreciated. All inquiries should be directed to didivsdragon.com.

Environmental consciousness is important. This book is printed on acid-free paper supplied by a Forest Stewardship Council-certified provider. The ink is chlorine-free.

First Edition 2022
Library of Congress Cataloging-in-Publication Data on file.
ISBN 979-8-9853213-5-7

The Dragon Egg

WORDS BY
DIDI DRAGON

PICTURES BY
MARIA MAU

Lucy could hardly fall asleep she was so excited for tomorrow. She had practiced all day to get ready for the Easter egg hunt. Her older brother Drew always seemed to get first place, but this year, Lucy was ready to win.

When morning finally came, all the neighborhood kids arrived at her house. While Dad explained the rules for the egg hunt, Lucy squinted at the backyard and squeezed the handle of her basket. The whistle blew, and Lucy ran.

She zipped through the yard, picking up as many eggs as possible. Her next stop was the far corner of the yard where her dad didn't always cut the grass. Sure enough, just behind a bush, she found the biggest egg she had ever seen.

It had so many colors and it sparkled in the sunlight. "I bet you this is the grand prize egg! I'll get so many points!" Lucy exclaimed. She hurried back to the middle of the yard to find more eggs.

Her dad blew the whistle again. "Everyone, hands up. No more picking up eggs!"

Everyone lined up to see who would win this year's egg hunt. Lucy peered over their baskets. She definitely felt like she could win. She looked in her own basket. Wait a second! Why were so many of her eggs opened? Who had eaten all the chocolate peanut butter cups?

"Lucy," Dad scolded, "you weren't supposed to eat the candy yet; you know that!"

He walked away to inspect the first basket in line. Lucy couldn't even respond, she was so confused. She put her hand on her grand prize egg. That was cracked open too!

She felt around the bottom of the basket to see if any eggs were still intact. Her fingers touched something cold and scaly. A frog!? If Drew was playing tricks on her again... She moved aside the eggs and wrappers.

Lucy had never seen anything like it. It was purple and had little glittering horns.

"I have to go to the bathroom!" Lucy shouted as she ran out of the line.

"But I need to count your eggs—leave your basket!" her dad said.

Lucy dashed inside to the bathroom. She locked the door and took a deep breath. Had her eyes been playing tricks on her? She peered at the basket but only saw a pile of plastic eggs and candy wrappers. But just then, a head popped out!

"Oh my gosh!" Lucy whispered excitedly. But what could it be? Lucy put out her hand. The creature sniffed her and then crawled onto her palm. Lucy could see it had purple scales, a gold spine and horns, claws and wings. It had wings! Lucy was absolutely in awe.

You are a Baby Dragon!

Lucy felt like the luckiest kid in the world. But she couldn't show anyone, not yet anyway. She wanted it to be her dragon, and if anyone found out, she was sure they were going to take it away. She looked at all the candy wrappers. "I'll call you Buttercup!"

Lucy put Buttercup back into the basket and went outside to the party. Drew had won the egg hunt. Lucy wasn't even upset like she would normally be. She'd get some food, take Buttercup up in her room and figure out a plan.

But just then her dog Gus came over and started sniffing her basket. Uh-oh! He could definitely smell the baby dragon! Keeping Buttercup a secret was going to be a much bigger challenge than Lucy had thought.

Lucy quickly grabbed a stick and threw it to the other side of the yard. "Go get it, Gus!" Phew, that was close! Lucy reached back into her basket. Buttercup wasn't there anymore! Lucy's stomach dropped. Where could her little dragon have gone?

"Owww!" screeched Miss May, leaping from her chair, her fruit salad flying from her hands. "Something pricked my bum!" Aha! It must have been Buttercup's horns. Lucy would have to train Buttercup to not charge at people or their bottoms.

Lucy looked around for Buttercup. Just then, Gus started barking again. A glimmer of purple streaked through the grass and then a brown tail followed. Oh no! Gus was chasing after the baby dragon!

Bark!!!

Buttercup and Gus both bolted through the dog door into the house. Lucy mentally added "practice running to catch bolting dragons" to her daily routine. She raced after them and threw open the door.

She saw her mom holding a very fussy Gus and frantically blowing out candles. "Lucy, someone lit all these candles. Help me blow them out!" Uh-oh. Dragons could breathe fire. Lucy wondered if she would be able to train Buttercup to breathe fire on command.

The sound was coming from the pantry. Mom paused. "Lucy, do you hear that?" Lucy held her breath. At least she didn't have to wonder what to feed her new dragon. "Of all the days to have a mouse in the pantry," Mom sighed. "Please finish blowing out the candles while I go get your father." Om-nom-nom-burrrrrp! An empty jar of crunchy peanut butter rolled into the kitchen.

Gus charged into the pantry. Pots and pans and cans crashed to the ground. Lucy covered her ears. Buttercup leaped out gracefully while Gus tripped after. How could she ever make a pug and dragon become friends?

The two critters bolted up the stairs with a pitter-patter of paws right into Drew's room. Lucy raced after them, expecting a crash, but when she burst through the door, the two were standing perfectly still.

Gus started to growl. Lucy knelt very slowly and reached to grab the snarling pug. "Gus, Buttercup is your friend. We need to be quiet so no one—" but it was too late! He charged toward Buttercup.

Nooooooo! Lucy shouted

Flip! Buttercup pounced on Gus's short nose, jumped into the air and flapped. The little dragon was flying! Of course it was flying, but Lucy had to gasp in wonder, and her eyes sparkled. Buttercup flew toward the wide-open skies beyond the window—bump!—but there was glass in the way. The little dragon landed on the sill and pressed its paw against the pane. Maybe it had a family out there somewhere.

Lucy really, really wanted a pet dragon. But she thought about what Buttercup wanted too. She opened the window. "Fly free," she whispered.

Buttercup flew close up to Lucy and licked the tip of her nose. Then the glittering dragon flew out and turned around once, as if to say thank-you. Lucy heard Drew coming up the stairs.

"What's going on?! And why are you in my room!" Drew exclaimed, trophy in hand. Lucy and Gus were looking out the window, watching Buttercup fly away over the party below. Lucy had forgotten entirely about the egg hunt.

"What are you guys looking at?" Drew squinted his eyes and looked into the distance. His mouth dropped open for a second, but then he shook his head: "Lucy, that's just a bird."

But Lucy just smiled as she waved goodbye to Buttercup.
They would see each other again, she just knew it.

See ya around, Buttercup!

Despite the fact that **Didi Dragon** is her name, she is not actually a dragon. It's just a name that as an author she made up. She didn't know much about dragons until her niece educated her and drew lots of drawings of them. If she'd ever find a baby dragon, she too would probably want it as a pet, but of course, set it free if that is what it wanted.

Oh yeah, she's written some other books like the bestsellers "Germs vs.Soap," "Cavities vs. Toothpaste," "Little Red Fox has Feelings" & "Rocket Girl." You can check them out on didivsdragon.com or on her Instagram @didivsdragon.

Maria Mau is a very curious illustrator who finds inspiration in the most unusual places: in the shadows of trees, in the howling of owls at night, in the clouds forming interesting shapes above her head, in all little and big animals she sees daily. She has many great tit bird friends that visit her on her terrace but she also finds the thought of having a baby dragon as a friend very appealing too.

She's previously collaborated with Didi Dragon on other books too, such as "Little Red Fox has Feelings" and "Rocket Girl." You can check out her artwork on mauillustration.com or on Instagram @mau.illustration.

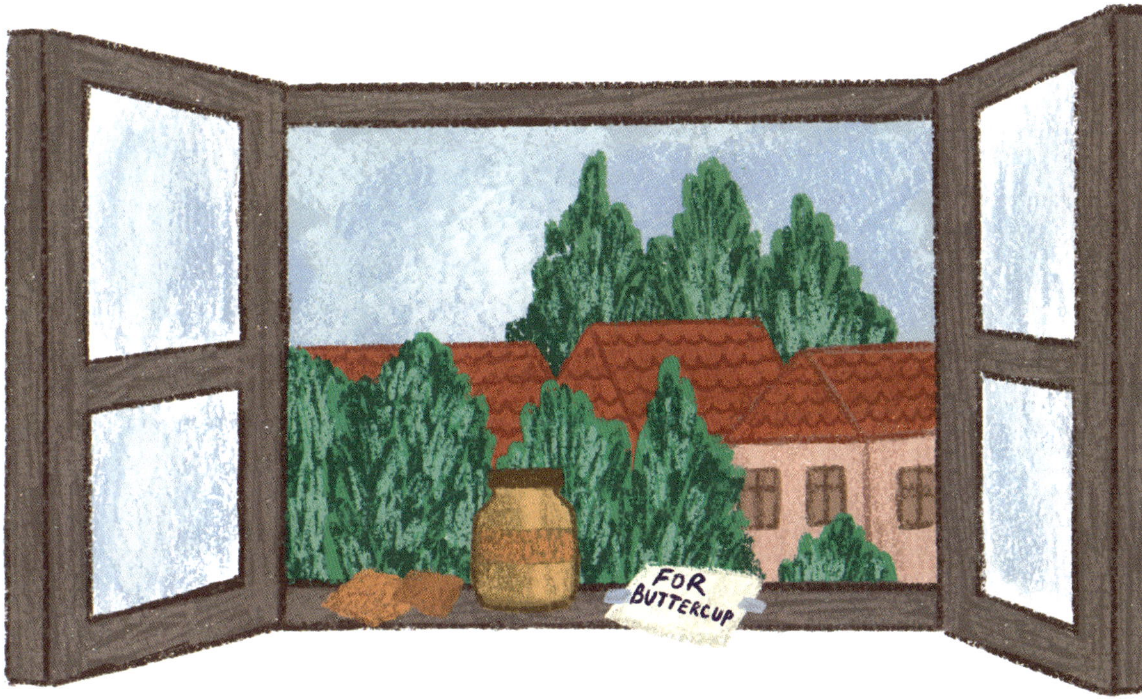
FOR
BUTTERCUP

Printed in Great Britain
by Amazon